Nostalgia Rue 

Presents

America's Ageism Syndrome:
The Ageism Crisis in America

By

Mitzi E. Monroe

A Twenty-First Century Assessment, Diagnosis and Social Initiatives to Change the Culture of Aging in America

First Edition

~ 2.0.1.8 ~

Believing
you are
less valuable
as an older person

is

Self

Discriminating

Ageism

prejudice or discrimination on the basis of a person's age

~ Mitzi E. Monroe, Nostalgia Rue

Nostalgia Rue 

Presents

America's Ageism Syndrome:
The Ageism Crisis in America

By

Mitzi E. Monroe

Nostalgia Rue's

America's Ageism Syndrome:
The Ageism Crisis in America

Contents..5

Words of Wisdom..7

Introduction: Ageism and The American Dream..8

The Assessment: The 50-Plus Quality of Life Evaluation 11

The Assessment...12
2008: The Great Recession: No Financial Bail Out for Boomers..................13
Aging Policies...17
Community...20

Diagnosis: Ageism Syndrome...22

Diagnostic Testing: Help!...23
The Results: America's Ageism Syndrome: The Ageism Crisis in America.........24
Symptomatic or Systemic?..25

Treatment Plan of Care: Community Initiatives for Changing the Culture of Ageism.....................27

- The Initiatives: I., II., III., IV..28
- Aging in Place Today! Bulletin...29
- Aging in Place Bill of Rights...30

Final Thoughts: A Call to Acton 31

Presents

America's Ageism Syndrome:
The Ageism Crisis in America

Founder/Publisher
Mitzi E. Monroe

Proof Reader
Gerry Richardson

9850 S. Maryland Parkway
Suite A-5, P.O. Box # 229
Las Vegas, Nevada 89183

Email: info@nostalgiarue.com
Website: www.nostalgiarue.com

Photo Credits:

Shea Homes for Vista Dora Brentwood, CA
Flickr, Wikimedia Commons and The Metropolitan Museum of Art
Adolphe Pierre-Louis, Professional Photographer
Mitzi E. Monroe, Nostalgia Rue

Disclaimer

Nostalgia Rue is a privately owned for-profit Multimedia publishing and entertainment company based in Las Vegas, Nevada. Sole proprietor, Mitzi E. Monroe, does not operate a non-profit, 501 (c) (3) organization. For more information, please explore my site and enjoy the possibilities!

~ Mitzi E. Monroe, Founder

Words of Wisdom

In a country well governed, poverty is something to be ashamed of.
In a country badly governed, wealth is something to be ashamed of. ~ <u>Confucius</u>

I think that ageism is a cultural illness; it's not a personal illness. ~ <u>Frances McDormand</u>

An individual has not started living until he can rise above the narrow confines of his
individualistic concerns to the broader concerns of all humanity. ~ <u>Martin Luther King, Jr.</u>

"He that would govern others, first should be the master of himself. " ~ <u>Phillip Massinger</u>

You don't make progress by standing on the sidelines, whimpering and complaining.
You make progress by implementing ideas. ~ <u>Shirley Chisholm</u>

You cannot hope to build a better world without improving the individuals. To that end, each of us must work
for his own improvement and, at the same time, share a general responsibility for all humanity, our particular
duty being to aid those to whom we think we can be most useful. ~ <u>Marie Curie</u>

In recognizing the humanity of our fellow beings, we pay ourselves the highest tribute. ~ <u>Thurgood Marshall</u>

We cannot seek achievement for ourselves and forget about progress and prosperity for our community.
Our ambitions must be broad enough to include the aspirations and needs of others,
for their sakes and for our own. ~ <u>Cesar Chavez</u>

America's Ageism Syndrome:
The Ageism Crisis in America

Introduction: Ageism and The American Dream

If you're wondering what ageism has to do with the American Dream? Everything! For the Baby Boomer generation born between 1946 and 1964, you may recall a time when middle and lower income post WWII parents and grandparents preached to your youth in the 1950s and 70s: go to college, work for a big U.S. manufacturer like General Motors or Ford for that grown up paycheck, health insurance and an old age pension as your pathway to the American Dream: Home ownership, a new car in the drive-way and a secured retirement pension, personal savings and social security benefits-the symbols of retirement prosperity. If you followed their edict and worked hard, your lay-a-way plan for the American dream would be paid off in thirty to forty years, just in time for your retirement.

The advice of those elders echoed the voice of author and American self-taught historian, James Truslow Adams (1878-1949), who first used or created the term "American Dream" in his 1931 book, "The Epic of America." The term coupled with hard work began spreading nationwide during the great depression's aspirational Hollywood golden age movies (1929-1959), celebrity magazines and books penetrating the consciousness of everyday Americans seeking a new and better future.

Decades later, the Baby Boomers' path to the American Dream in the 21st century has been challenged by the loss of "Made in America" middle income factory jobs, early lay-offs for career professionals deemed too old, the loss or depletion of retirement funds during the great recession of 2008, and low paying post retirement jobs. These norms in today's uncertain economic climate have disrupted the ability to plan for the golden years.

Post the great recession, older persons age fifty and up are experiencing a job depression. The loss of pensions and a social security system that was structured to be supplementary to personal savings and pensions have put the American Dream out of reach for the average middle age and older person.

"It's called the American Dream b'cause you have to be asleep to believe it." ~ George Carlin, Comedian

For most African-American descendants of slaves or any person born into poverty, statistically, work has not yielded a sufficient income to invest in opportunities for income equality. The American Dream is a myth in their minds.

"We don't see any American dream. We've experienced only the American nightmare." ~ Malcolm X, Human Rights Activist

Nostalgia Rue's

Introduction: Ageism and The American Dream

Therefore, older persons experiencing either pre or post retirement years have not had the means to fully recover or build adequate savings due to sporadic gaps in cashflow; again, disappearing pensions, housing foreclosures and bankruptcies. Without a return on sweat equity that affords a person a financial safety net or a family can rely on, the picture is bleak. And most older adult's pride prevents them from exposing their debt in fear they will become a burden to their family. The shame for a situation that is not all or part their fault has increased significantly in suicide deaths due to depression and despair for persons age 45 and older.

The American Foundation for Suicide Prevention's 2016 report concluded the highest suicide rate, 19.72%, was amongst adults age 45 to 54 years old. The second highest rate, 18.98%, is for age 85 or older. The U.S. Census Bureau warned, if the elderly suicide rates remain the same, more than 11,000 lives will be lost per year due to suicide.

Without a nationwide plan to tear down the barriers of ageism that render older persons invisible and ignore an aging culture that denies there is a long term care crisis in America, the crisis will only exacerbate the negative quality of life issues hitting the largest age wave in American history, and age wave of persons turning age 65 and Medicare eligible at a rate of 10,000 per day since January 2011. And that is just the tip when you consider the entire spectrum of persons living longer.

The negative effects of ageism, whether the attitude be a by product of ignorance or an assumed stereotypical judgment, has everything to do with this segment of our population seeing their American dream fade away and disappear resulting in a bleak future without rescue at the most vulnerable period of their lives.

Ageism is the only "ism" in our ethos that has not been addressed socially beyond lip service to change the culture of aging in America inter-generationally, through policy changes or through local community calls to action.

Nostalgia Rue's

America's Ageism Syndrome:
The Ageism Crisis in America

Introduction: Ageism and The American Dream

There are many great advocates, authors, and I'm certain, individuals working in Long Term Care who are doing their best daily to be of service. But tearing down the build up of ageism's ugly realities will require more than thinking about, selfishly excusing the obvious, and feeling you have no incentive to deal with it puts yourself and everyone in harm's way sooner or later. What you ignore today will be your inheritance as an older person ,should you live to grow old. It is a moral responsibility to be a part of the solution.

Personally, I'm appalled at what I've witnessed, observed and read about, in regard to, how our older citizens are treated or mistreated through complete disregard. It's disrespectful at best. For example, most recently I watched a very popular cable entertainment host make derogatory jokes about a famous renown actor being too old to present a prestigious industry award. I've also witnessed a young big box store cashier dismiss three older customers who were next in line for a younger customer; possibly friends in line? And there are plenty of TV shows and movies where older women are not cast as the love interest of a similar age male character. And lastly, I had a private duty client whose wealthy son blamed his parents for being old, not having retirement savings and berated them for needing his monetary support.

In my *Aging in Place Lifestyle Book-A-Zine (March 2018),* I share a famous ageist statement that went viral as quoted at a 2007 Stanford University event, where Mark Zuckerberg, CEO and Founder of Facebook was quoted telling the attendees: "*Young people are just smarter*," to justify not hiring persons over age 30. I guess he didn't attend the employment and discrimination class.

Without a dialogue that puts actions behind our findings to bridge the realities of aging and living longer, ageism's effects will impact the present, negate our past and influence future generations to be ageist, culturally, from childhood to death.

Discussing the ills and shame of ageism is not an easy discussion to have. But we must. We are beyond pointing fingers. We are all accountable for this mess. So let's move on and get to work.

This book will not only address the problems that have plagued our growing 50-plus population, I wrote this book to propose a call to action and suggest diverse ideas to combat ageism and begin the process of changing the culture of aging for an all age thinking community from local to national, in that order, in the last pages and final thoughts section of this book.

I would have never written this book without ending it with a help me, help you to help us agenda. We can no longer remain silent. The issues and concerns that plague our elders is not your problem, it's our problem.

Nostalgia Rue's

America's Ageism Syndrome:

The Ageism Crisis in America

The Assessment:

The 50-Plus Quality of Life Evaluation

By

Mitzi E. Monroe

America's Ageism Syndrome:
The Ageism Crisis in America

The Assessment:
The 50-Plus Quality of Life Evaluation

When I was researching for my new books: *Aging in Place Lifestyle Book-A-Zine and the two Aging in Place - Long Term Care Symposiums in Print,* I found my voice and purpose.

That purpose is advocating for an all age thinking agenda using my voice to eradicate ageism for persons aging in place via my pen. I even coined a term, "Ageism Syndrome," to define my findings. It's easier for people to understand a problem if there's a word or term and definition to concretely describe what it is you're talking about.

Initially *America's Ageism Syndrome: The Ageism Crisis in America* was only a keynote address to be defined and used in context to the *Aging in Place –LTC Symposiums in Print*. The definition really defines what the social barriers are to addressing the long term care crisis in America. The definition confirmed there was much more that needed to be said with a call to action proposed on the subject.

As a 55-year old baby boomer with thirty-five years of experience in medical and non-medical long term care, my generation, the largest age wave in U.S. history, has no national or local plan of action for surviving an "extended life" post retirement.

But how do you inform your community grocers, educators, librarians, politicians, neighbors, elder care professionals, employers, our youth, caregivers, our media and our churches, etc. that we have a long term care crisis whose gate keeper is ageism? The long list of biases against older persons puts their well-being in harms way, breeds fear of aging and dictates a negative impact on the culture of aging for everyone in our society.

To prove there is a nationwide ageism syndrome, I've developed a 50-Plus Quality of Life Evaluation which assesses discrimination against all older persons and their economic recovery status post the great recession of 2008 to present. This evaluation has three key categories to justify we cannot change the culture of aging in the United States until we:

- **Assess** the symptomatic characteristics of ageism that impacts our older population.
- **Diagnose** the systemic signs of ageism.
- Adopt a **<u>Plan of Care Treatment</u>** (Call to Action) for changing ageist attitudes and behaviors toward older people to develop a culture change that will engage an all age thinking agenda in our communities.

America's Ageism Syndrome:
The Ageism Crisis in America

The Assessment:
The 50-Plus Quality of Life Evaluation

2008: The Great Recession: "No Bail Out" for Boomers

It's been a decade since the great recessions impact hi-jacked wallets, foreclosed homes and trended bankruptcies in the United States.

Today the remnants of that financial crisis still haunts the baby boomer generations confusion of "WTF" happened to their inheritance? They were promised to inherit the American Dream bigger and better that the great generation. The greatest generation (1910-1924) promised them a college education and hard work coupled with their late parents family home, savings and a low-mileage retirement car would secure their future retirement.

The Insured Retirement Institute (IRI) Reports:

- Only 24% of Baby Boomers are confident they will have enough savings to last throughout retirement, down from 36% in 2012.

- Only 55% of Baby Boomers have *any* money saved for retirement. In fairness, however, one in four Baby Boomers expects significant income from an employer-provided pension.

- 59% of Baby Boomers cite Social Security as a major source of their retirement income.

- 65% of Baby Boomers are worried about future changes to Social Security.

- Only 43% of Baby Boomers are satisfied with how their lives are going from an economic perspective.

- 26% of Baby Boomers don't plan to retire until age 70 or later.

- Only 22% of Baby Boomers believe they are doing a good job of preparing financially for retirement.

- Only 27% of Baby Boomers believe they will have enough money for healthcare expenses.

The reality is: No generation went unscathed by the great recession. The path to recovery appears to be a wilderness too dense to navigate when you consider any person lucky enough to have savings pre-great recession that took ten or more years to acquire lost up to 50% or all of their balance during the financial crisis. Plus there were/are management fees and penalties to cash out a portion of their money or close those accounts to strategize an urgent survival plan.

America's Ageism Syndrome:
The Ageism Crisis in America

The Assessment:
The 50-Plus Quality of Life Evaluation

2008: The Great Recession: "No Bail Out" for Boomers

Finding another professional salaried job, after the recession, and outliving another ten or more years on a full-time job to catch up to or exceed their lost savings alludes many baby boomers, but more so for the boomers in their 50s and 60s who have no recovery in sight. The new retirement plan includes working into their seventies or indefinitely just to manage the essentials of room and board.

National studies and the National Alliance to End Homelessness released an April 2017 report that 2.4% of homeless older adults age 50-to-64 years old have a higher rate of homelessness due to their ineligibility to qualify for safety net programs, such as: Subsidized housing, Medicare and social security benefits due to age or not knowing when they are eligible. There is an estimate that over 45,000 homeless seniors are living on the streets nationwide with college degrees and do not have a mental illness. That is another misnomer that everyone who hasn't recovered from the economic crisis of 2008 is also lazy, not trying hard enough to find a good paying job or is just too old to be productive.

Regardless of someone's mental stability or defined crisis, it is time to stop blaming persons fifty and older for aging, it is time to acknowledge the ills of ageist attitudes and behaviors to realize we are living in a time that is very different from the post WWII spirit of rebuilding jobs, families and community.

We are experiencing fewer American factories and affordable vocational programs where non-degreed persons can earn a middle class income.

It would not be a bad idea to use the past as a starting point now. My assessment of what is vs. what isn't, provides evidence things will most likely never return to what could have been for the baby boomer generation. The largest population of retirement age persons in U.S. history thus far has a legacy that headlines a triple theme: The great recession, a long term care crisis and no bailout recovery plan for boomers.

There is a reason why there are so many middle-age low-wage older workers at big box retail chains, fast food restaurants and non-medical caregiver agency jobs. Jobs that were once rite of passage jobs for teenagers. The average pay for these jobs are $15,000 to $22,000 per year full-time. Many of these workers must supplement these jobs with food stamps and any other helpline they have to invest time to find to make ends meet. The middle-middle and lower middle classes continue towards economic extinction.

2008: **The Great Recession:** "No Bail Out" for Boomers

Another misnomer: Not everyone on food stamps or working low-wage jobs are there because they lack a college education, career experience or drive. Persons age fifty and older are not hired for their degrees, resume or knowledge. They're not hired or they're fired and/or laid-off first because companies discriminate based on their interpersonal or personal judgment of older persons. The two biggest reasons being, employers feel they are:

1. Less productive.
2. More costly to the employers benefit plans.

The lowest wage earners in the country with too many at the end of their most productive years in life and work paid taxes to help bail out the banks and Wall Street with no reciprocation.

The same year of the great recession, Wall Street paid out 18 billion in bonuses. Where are the bail outs for post recession older American's struggling to make their ends meet?

There are plenty of documentaries, books and sporadic interviews on national news networks over the years pointing out the ageist indignities of older persons suffering the consequences of a financial crisis, statistics are bulleted lists and political debates are had with no rescue for the oldest segment of our population due to the great recession of 2008 and the ageism that persists.

The persons great generation who are living today are between 94-108 years old in 2018. If they are living today and they too have no solid safety net, and their children have the financial means, 10% of their boomer children are financially supporting them and their children. Which means it's possible, their boomer children may not have enough savings for their own retirement.

We have a disaster with 10,000 people a day eligible to retire. For example, a person may have enough funds upon retirement to move into an assistant living facility of their choice. If a time comes when they exhaust their pension and/or savings, a lack of personal funds to supplement Medicare, they will be faced with having to find another affordable aging in place option.

The bottom-line, people are living longer and we as a nation both locally and nationally need to stop identifying the problems outlined in this chapter and take seriously the aging crisis we've been warned about: "The graying of America age wave," since the mid 1980s. We're there and we're overdue for a call to action.

2008: **The Great Recession:** "No Bail Out" for Boomers

Go Bank Rates data reports:

- 1 in 3 Americans have no savings.

- 42% of Americans have less than $10,000 saved for retirement. An increase from 23% reported in 2016.

- 16% of working adults have $300,000 or more in retirement savings. Usually not enough for a twenty year or longer lifespan.

The welfare and well-being of every living person should not be a moral dilemma for any generation. What you can do for today's older generation will teach us to how to help future generations, including your own.

Assessment: More than not, too many of America's pre-and-post retirement baby boomers age 50 years and older are not prepared to plan for a short or long term retirement. Low wage post retirement jobs are not enough to maintain a pre-retirement lifestyle that includes a mortgage, credit card debt or average rent that is challenged by the typical single person social security benefit of $1,400.00 and couples $2,400.00.

Data also indicates elders have little or no health care coverage or emergency funds to rely on. Without question, we need a national solution. A call to action. The culture of aging must change locally and nationally to prevent, recover and help older persons maintain a reasonable quality of life into their later years.

America's Ageism Syndrome:

The Ageism Crisis in America

The Assessment:

The 50-Plus Quality of Life Evaluation

Aging Policies

With thirty-five years experience in elder care, I can't confess I know everything about all the components to political policies on aging from Washington to anywhere else U.S.A. More importantly, I will write this piece on aging policies from the perspective of a caregiver based on what I've observed on the front lines of long term care, what I've heard from care receivers and their family members assisting them to navigate the aging policies.

My assessment will be indicative of how services can be improved by what is lacking in layman terms based on my research to express my findings in ways anyone reads this will be able to relate to, is my hope.

First I'd like to share a little history of our aging policies and entitlement programs:

A Brief History of Aging in America:

The United States borrowed and formed the aging services concept by using the Elizabethan Poor Law, a poor relief act, that was passed in England in 1601. The law was a system to help the old and frail or out of work poor.

In the last 200 years the United States has seen an increase in life expectancy from the mid-40s to the late 70s today. With advancements in hygiene protocols, vaccines and medical treatments people have a lifespan of 75 to 100-plus years today.

Unfortunately, the aging services that include home delivered meals, senior centers and medically necessary care benefits have struggled in recent decades to adapt to longer lifespans, the delivery of five day meal plans vs. seven days a week, long term care custodial programs and outreach services and advocacy campaigns have failed to advocate against ageism in their unique platforms in partnership with the medical industry and their communities at large.

The Ageism Crisis in America

The Assessment:
The 50-Plus Quality of Life Evaluation

Aging Policies

Between 1935 and 1965 the U.S. government enacted the following laws and entitlement programs:

1935: President Franklin D. Roosevelt signs the Social Security Act of 1935. Social Security was established to supplement retirement savings and pensions. Like today's post great recession, the Great Depression highlighted the challenges of aging that includes high rates of unemployment for persons age 50-60, lost savings and financially challenged long term care programs that excludes the lower middle class poor population.

1940: Ida May Fuller of Brattleboro, Vermont received the first social security check, dated January 31, 1940 for $22.54.

1952: Congress appropriated the first federal funds for social service programs for older Americans.

1965: The Older Americans Act (OAA), Medicaid and Medicare was signed into law by President Lyndon B. Johnson.

1967: The Age Discrimination in Employment Act of 1967 (ADEA) is a US labor law that forbids employment discrimination against anyone at least 40 years of age in the United States. In 1967, the bill was signed into law by President Lyndon B. Johnson.

1975: The Age Discrimination Act of 1975 prohibits discrimination on the basis of age in programs and activities receiving federal financial assistance. The Act, which applies to all ages, permits the use of certain age distinctions and factors other than age that meet the Act's requirements.

America's Ageism Syndrome:
The Ageism Crisis in America

The Assessment:
The 50-Plus Quality of Life Evaluation

Aging Policies

If I were asked what U.S. policies or entitlement programs need to be revised or added, in the 21st century, I'd list:

1. **Ageism Advocacy-Outreach Campaigns** (Intergenerational Pilot Programs)**:** We need a two-year movement to educate school age children and every adult age group about attitudes and behaviors to prevent discrimination against older people based on their age, stereotypes and judgments.

2. **Consumer-Directed Care** (Custodial Care)**:** More people are aging in place by choice or without choice in their private homes due to limited personal incomes in cities or in rural areas with limited or no nearby resources. As more people age in place they will require financial support to help family or caregivers provide non-medical quality of life services. Those services will include activities of daily living like bathing, companionship, errands and meal prep that their entitlement programs; medically necessary services do not cover.

3. **Professional Caregiving** (Training/Vocational, Incomes & Flexible Jobs)**:** Rebuild work training vocational programs in skilled nursing facilities for certified nurse aides to bridge medical and non-medical skill sets for in-home care with living wages above $14 per hour.

4. **Family Caregiving** (Respite, Pay & Training)**:** Provide professional training and financial relief programs for family caregivers who must work F/T at home to help a loved one age in place with care as a safety net.

5. **Nutrition** (Meal Programs, Buying Food & Preparation)**:** Extend meals on wheels to 6 or 7 days per week.

6. **Companionship/In-Home Adult Day Care:** Extend adult day care services for in-home rehabilitation care for seniors who may be isolated and shut-in due to an in-home recovery period. Data proves social engagement helps to lessen or prevent depression and promote physical healing.

7. **Hospice Care** (End of Life Care)**:** Paid assistance for 2-4 hours of custodial care based on need.

Assessment: To better serve the new old age we must unlearn old methods for a new approach to delivering service and support methods based on the actual realities of aging today.

Nostalgia Rue's

America's Ageism Syndrome:
The Ageism Crisis in America

The Assessment:
The 50-Plus Quality of Life Evaluation

Community

Over the last four decades the community spirit has been fractured and changed from city-wide pride that bonded fellow locals with a mutual interests to come together by way of large multifarious family gatherings at least twice a year with a neutral sponsor, the city or state. These annual events were family friendly gatherings where you interacted with your fellow city dwellers no matter your race or economic status. You were free to come and have a good time. Local pride was at an all-time high.

Local media was 80% dedicated to local content and 20% national. After all, Walter Cronkite, David Brinkley and Harry Reasoner provided the global world news on the three national broadcast networks.

Your in-state news programs introduced small and large local businesses with a well-rounded overview of what's new, what's old and what's about to happen where you lived. I can recall weekly guest commentaries by locals to keep you in the loop of that community spirit and agenda.

Today, there is a cultural shift from us to them. In the last two decades, everything from charities to health care organizations and small franchises that serve the elder care marketplace have become so competitive they have established tribes that are extremely territorial of their space due to monetary special interests.

That lack of reciprocity out of the normal circles, openness to new thinking and opportunities has been a reflection of why the culture of business practices have made it difficult when it shouldn't be to improve communication channels in the best interests of older persons. And small solopreneur ventures have a difficult time seeing a return on their registration fees, marketing fees and social networking out-of-pocket costs.

The divisions, extreme tactics to keep the competition at bay is also preventing our seniors from accessing and receiving diversified services and information not all behemoths can not provide, ever due to their pay structure, etc.

To face these challenges, we need to learn community 1-on-1 again to find there are individuals, groups and enterprising entrepreneurs ignoring the status quo and doing what they can to keep the current affairs at bay.

So yes, there are campaigns to change the culture of aging, educate the communities about the long term care crisis and the negative impact of ageism. Unfortunately, everyone, whether you're an elder care professional or Joe Pick Your Nose, it is of the utmost importance we take notice of these campaigns and participate. I am amazed at how many people have not heard of the Silver Tsunami, age wave or that there is a long term crisis in America.

Nostalgia Rue's

America's Ageism Syndrome:
The Ageism Crisis in America

The Assessment:
The 50-Plus Quality of Life Evaluation

Community

It is imperative we reach out to one another one-on-one and as a group. We have to stop ignoring calls to action.

We are all part of the human race tribe. If we keep ignoring the truths that are in view, the long term crisis will be inherited by everyone as is: broken.

We must unlearn the attitudes and behaviors that have not served us well in the mature marketplace. A community is only as strong as its body of people living there.

The older population is counting on "us" to be the community that will join together in one voice to be there for them throughout their later years. It will be hard to change the culture of aging but it's not impossible.

If nothing more, change the culture of aging for yourself. What you gain from it will be passed down to benefit future generations.

We can't afford another century of repeating the same infractions on humanity.

Nostalgia Rue's 

America's Ageism Syndrome:
The Ageism Crisis in America

The Diagnosis: Ageism Syndrome
The 50-Plus Quality of Life Evaluation

By

Mitzi E. Monroe

Nostalgia Rue's

America's Ageism Syndrome:
The Ageism Crisis in America

The Diagnosis: Ageism Syndrome
The 50-Plus Quality of Life Evaluation

Diagnostic Testing: Help!

Below are categories in which ageism against older persons can be identified through everyday occurrences listed by example. Ageism can be discrimination that is based on a judgment or stereotype, an attitude or behavior towards a person because of their age.

Communication:

- Patronize them.
- Talking at them instead of with them.
- Talking too loud assuming an older person is hard of hearing.
- Tell them vs. ask them.
- Being rude and dismissive.
- Ask a question and not let them answer.

Community:

- No financial crisis recovery plan.
- No call to action to eradicate ageism.
- No urgency to change aging policies..
- No reinforcement of discrimination laws.

Businesses/Jobs/Work:

- Eased out of job for their age.
- Won't hire due to their age rather than offer job based on their resume and experience.
- Disregards discrimination laws.

Family:

- Treats them like children.
- Blames them for getting old: "You're walking too slow!"
- Impatient and rushes them to complete tasks.
- Makes them feel guilty for needing financial support.

Social Stereotypes:

- Shunned
- Ignored
- Their age group only wants to be home.
- Assume they have no interests.
- Assume their age (#) is a characteristic of their abilities.
- Assume they have no ambitions.
- Judge an older person is homeless because they're an old failure or incapable of being productive.
- Being old means they have dementia or Alzheimer's.

Media:

- Send the messages youth is everything.
- Assumes everyone wants to be younger instead of their age.
- Constantly assume everyone of a certain age is not okay with wrinkles or gray hair with ads that only promotes youth in a pill or bottle.
- Programs that highlight the different stages of maturity.
- Lack solutions or advocacy programming.
- Town Hall Meetings and specials highlighting the voices of people aging.
- A fair ratio of programs for older audiences.

America's Ageism Syndrome:
The Ageism Crisis in America

The Diagnosis: Ageism Syndrome
The 50-Plus Quality of Life Evaluation

Diagnostic Test Results: Ageism Syndrome:

A systemic social zombie like state of persons who are unaware of how their negative behaviors, lack of empathy and age biases against a person or group older or younger than themselves negatively impacts the quality of life and state of well-being of every person in our society. ~ Mitzi E. Monroe

 Nostalgia Rue's

The Diagnosis:

America's Ageism Syndrome: The Ageism Crisis in America
The 50-Plus Quality of Life Evaluation

Symptomatic or Systemic:

Former head of the Columbia Advisory Committee on Aging, renowned Psychiatrist Robert N. Butler (1927-2010) coined the term "ageism" in 1969 to define the discrimination on the grounds of someone's age.

Nearly half a century later, the ageist attitudes and behaviors that identify prejudice and discrimination towards older persons (and younger) in the 21st century, are being ignored in mainstream culture. Although there are discrimination laws on the books, the Age Discrimination in Employment Act of 1967 and the Age Discrimination Act of 1975 prohibited discrimination on the basis of age in the U.S. Yet, these civil rights laws, corporate diversity training and sparse community outreach efforts have not scratched the moral conscience in mainstream culture.

How do we define a culture of aging in America in the 21st century that has no local or national leadership to push a call to action agenda or new aging policies that provide safety nets in response to a phenomenal indifference that is rooted in ageist acts against older persons?

My term for this phenomenon is ageism syndrome: A new term I've coined that groups all the characteristics and the dysfunctional societal affects of ageism's biases, stereotypes and isms that identify nuanced judgments, attitudes and behaviors that discriminate against older persons (and younger) framed by a cultural norm that violates the civil rights and quality of life for persons age 50 or older.

I define ageism syndrome as a systemic social zombie like state of persons who are unaware of how their negative behaviors, lack of empathy and age biases against a person or group older or younger than themselves negatively impacts the quality of life and state of well-being of every person in our society. ~ Mitzi E. Monroe

Ageism syndrome is both symptomatic and systemic. Symptomatic because there is a lack of empathy for data and signs that substantiate that older persons are experiencing increased homelessness, food insecurities, limited or no health care coverage and financial vulnerabilities repeatedly. Systemic because the complexities of our generations long term care crisis affects millions of older persons due to an outdated health care system that was created many decades before when the older population was smaller, had a shorter life span in a time when retirement most often includes Medicare, social security, personal savings and a pension that is not guaranteed today.

Ageism is a barrier that prevents a new thinking about real life situations for older persons in our blind spot.

The Ageism Crisis in America

The Diagnosis:

America's Ageism Syndrome: The Ageism Crisis in America

The 50-Plus Quality of Life Evaluation

Symptomatic or Systemic:

Some historians claim ageism began during the industrial revolutions (1760-late 1800s) when manufacturing of products, services and transportation (steamboats, etc.) offered swifter trading, consumer consumption and job development. The pre-factory system was the first step to formal jobs that changed the family dynamic in the 18th and 19th centuries.

I personally believe ageism syndrome has always existed as long as man has been on the planet. Looking back for centuries when the first European settlers came to North America, there had to be ageism harbored by resentment with regard to the care of the very young and the older family members in terms of how difficult it had to be to keep them safe, alive and compensate for their lack of or limited physical resources to contribute to the entire colonies daily survival in the new world.

Not only is it difficult to imagine the emotional and physical challenges for settlers to organize colonies in the new world with respect to the Native American Indian's protection of life as they knew it in their native land, no life in the undeveloped wilderness could be easy for any inhabitants of the new world. Lives were shorter due to sickness, childbirth was life threatening, communicable diseases, hard physical labor, compromised immune systems in harsh elements and poor hygiene. All factors could generate an early on-set of aging, shorter lives and a symptomatic and systemic ageist culture that was ingrained on an aging segment of society way before the industrial revolution.

Our aging culture of disregarding the cold hard facts that living longer has not been met with national acknowledgment beyond what we all know: not enough Americans are financially prepared for retirement.

Without a national plan to include middle class and poverty-stricken persons with innovative modern solutions the greatest age wave in American history will all be poverty-stricken and the poor will suffer a more devastating life challenging survival.

It sounds horrific. I hope not. But it will take more than hope to change the long term care crisis that is already in existence.

Nostalgia Rue's 

America's Ageism Syndrome:
The Ageism Crisis in America

Treatment Plan of Care:
Community Initiatives for Changing the Culture of Ageism

By

Mitzi E. Monroe

Nostalgia Rue's

America's Ageism Syndrome:
The Ageism Crisis in America

Treatment Plan of Care:
Community Initiatives for Changing the Culture of Ageism

The Initiatives: Phase I., II., III., IV.

I have established an informal voluntary DIY Community Initiatives for Aging in Place advocacy for any community of individuals or groups of people to do something once or routinely to make a difference for older persons aging in place. For those of you who are interested in being part of the solution, I've outlined four phases of the initiatives. If you'd like new updates and how to guides for helping out retirees in your community, visit: www.nostalgiarue.com and subscribe to the Aging in Place Today! Bulletin for monthly issues to stay current.

The Nostalgia Rue Community Initiatives for Aging in Place is a companion to the Aging in Place -Long Term Care Symposiums in Print. My contribution will be a communication platform to learn, reciprocate information, and outreach.

Please take the opportunity to review the information and visit Nostalgia Rue at: www.nostalgiarue.com.

To subscribe to the Aging in Place Today! Bulletin for great ideas, how to guides and updates on what's new, what's old and what's about to happen to help you and me advocate for an "all age thinking" community anywhere U.S.A.

The benefits of a collective long term commitment can be passed down generation to generation.

Phase I: Community Initiatives for Aging in Place
Phase II: Community Pledge
Phase III: Community Eldercare Fund
Phase IV: The Festival of Life®

America's Ageism Syndrome:
The Ageism Crisis in America

Treatment Plan of Care:
Community Initiatives for Changing the Culture of Ageism

Aging in Place Today! Bulletin

Get initiative details in every bulletin (Phase I-IV):

In continuance with the Aging in Place-Long Term Care Symposium in Print, I have published a Community Initiative for Aging in Place monthly newsletter entitled, "Nostalgia Rue's Aging in Place Today! Bulletin," for anyone, anywhere USA, to join together (informally).

A monthly bulletin that shares important aging in place news updates, creative ideas, and tips you can use individually or in group settings to set small but attainable goals to help a single person or a few people at a time embrace the culture and benefits of an all age thinking community.

Subscribe to Receive Your First Bulletin:

Visit: www.nostalgiarue.com and follow the subscriber instructions. The bulletins are $3/month.

A PDF is delivered via e-mail every month!

www.nostalgiarue.com
Copyright © 2018 by Mitzi E. Monroe

Nostalgia Rue's

Aging in Place Bill of Rights

Care Receivers', Eldercare Professionals' & Familial Caregivers'

Caregivers and Care Receivers Have the Right To:

1. Receive access to long term care training, industry acknowledgment and information to safely provide consumer-directed quality service to care for recipients aging in place.

2. Expect mutual respect and support for the challenges of private care giving.

3. Protect their privacy, their assets and the financial terms of their agreement without compromising their client-care receiver relationship.

4. Have time-off, breaks and respite to take care of self.

5. Say no, set boundaries and ask for help to safely perform aging in place care.

6. Provide or receive care and services, in-home, as long as it is financially feasible, physically safe and emotionally possible. When it is not possible, the caregivers have the responsibility to find alternatives, such as a residential care facility, that can meet the required needs to continue aging in place on another level of care.

7. Modify their home to provide a safe and livable home to age in place safely.

8. Request and receive culturally appropriate services to accommodate the care receivers' lifestyle preferences.

9. Seek and easily access specialized professional services, such as with interior and exterior home modifications, household management and in-home care services like hospice and consumer directed private-pay caregivers at varied stages of aging to acknowledge both the concerns of the caregivers and care receivers for open communication and roles in the best delivery of non-medical and prescribed physician plans of care.

10. Request, participate in and expect new long term care industry standards that include a clearing house with a community outreach center that welcomes nationwide participation that bridges the gap between medical, non-medical care and manpower for unexpected emergencies, occurrences and in-home social engagement programs that acknowledges and includes older persons aging in place in their private homes.

www.nostalgiarue.com
Copyright © 2018 by Mitzi E. Monroe

Nostalgia Rue's

The Ageism Crisis in America

Final Thoughts: A Call to Acton

Dear Readers,
Thank you for purchasing Nostalgia Rue's new book: **America's Ageism Syndrome:** The Ageism Crisis in America.

This book was not written to preach to you. So I ask your forgiveness and patience if that's the impression I've made. But just as importantly, older persons need our help to age in place. The main media and our long term care system has good intentions. But even hell is paved with good intentions.

What's not normally heard about are the actual cases in which there are too many people being added to data much too often about aging in debt and the long term care crisis without any call to action to fix it.

My call to action was designed where you didn't need to join an elaborate time intensive scheme to participate. An act of kindness is a good call to action. There are many friends, family and strangers who may need the kind of assistance to survive that is not your own situation. No excuses.

Reaching out individually or as a group effort can be life changing for a person in dire straits. Dire straights can be food insecurities, monetary losses, loneliness coupled with depression and poor health.

I have four phases to my shared initiatives to offer a starting point where you can determine your own proposals or feel free to follow me for detailed ideas and how to implement those ideas in your community.

Visit Nostalgia Rue at: www.nostalgiarue.com to subscribe to Aging in Place Today! Bulletin and learn more about what's new, what's old and what's about to happen!

Best!

Mitzi E. Monroe, Founder/Publisher

Website: www.nostalgiaruue.com
Email: info@nostalgiarue.com

Nostalgia Rue's

Eldercare Professionals' of America

Aging In Place - Long Term Care Symposium In Print

First Edition

America's Ageism Syndrome:

The Ageism Crisis in America

By

Mitzi E. Monroe

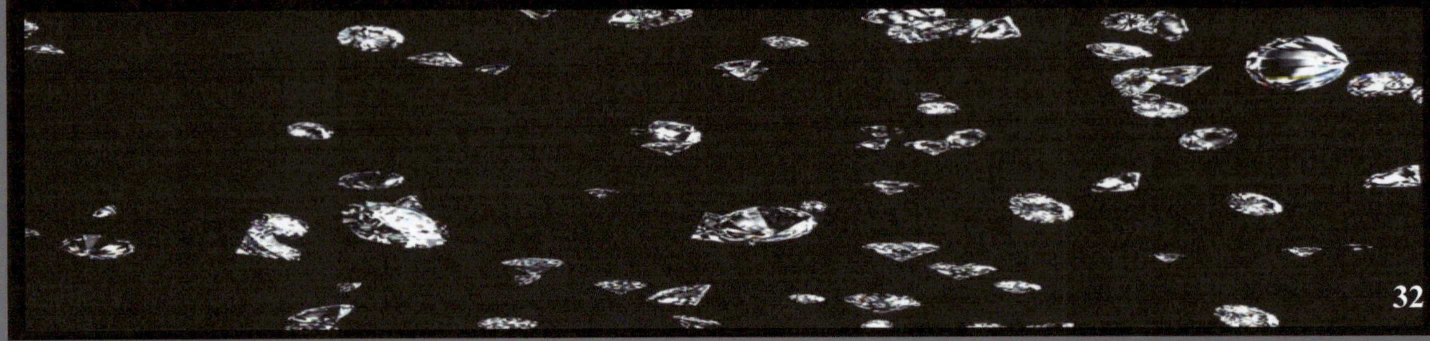